SUSAN OWEN AND ANGELA HAINE

Discovering
Walks in Surrey

GW00371225

SHIRE PUBLICATIONS LTD

Contents

The maps were drawn by Richard G. Holmes. The cover photograph of Shere is by Cadbury Lamb.

Printed in Great Britain by C. I. Thomas & Sons (Haverfordwest) Ltd, Press Buildings, Merlins Bridge, Haverfordwest, Dyfed SA61 1XF.

Introduction

This book of walks in Surrey has been completely revised and some of the extensions to the walks have been deleted or altered for various reasons and more appropriate ones inserted. Many changes have taken place in the countryside in the ten years since we first devised these walks. The opening of the M25 was the most significant man-made change, of course, but the October 1987 hurricane has changed the look of many hills and slopes almost beyond recognition and it will take a few years before the scars have faded. In some cases new vistas have been opened up.

Not all the changes have been bad: we were pleasantly surprised by the number of broken stiles that have been replaced and the new signposts that have appeared.

Ordnance Survey maps (186 and 187) cover the area of the walks and for those without their own transport, Surrey County Council have produced a free map 'Buses in Surrey', showing bus routes, railway lines, long distance paths and open spaces. This can be obtained from libraries and tourist information centres, or from the Transportation Planning Unit, Surrey County Council, Room 311, County Hall, Penrhyn Road, Kingston-upon-Thames, Surrey.

As regards footwear, some attempt has been made to indicate the amount of mud to be encountered, but we have found that boots or wellingtons are best for winter walking when the bridleways and farm paths can become churned up by horses and cattle; even in the summer, after prolonged rain, some paths can be impassable with ordinary shoes.

We hope that you will enjoy your rambles in this beautiful county.

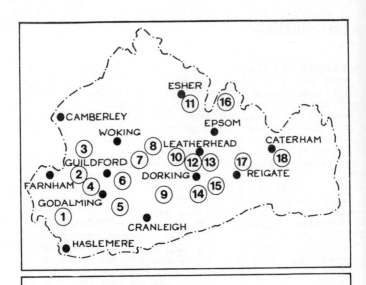

KEY TO SKETCH MAPS

✳	START OF WALK
◄━·━···	ROUTE OF WALK
Ⓟ	CAR PARK
═══	ROAD
≡≡≡≡≡	TRACK
━ ━ ━	OTHER FOOTPATHS
■	BUILDING
⌗	CHURCH
P.O.	POST OFFICE
P.H.	PUBLIC HOUSE
∿∿∿	RIVER OR STREAM
⬭	WATER FEATURE
┿●┿	RAILWAY AND STATION
)(	BRIDGE

4

1. Frensham Little Pond, the Devil's Jumps and Yagden Hill

Distance: 7 or 6 miles.
Grid reference: 859418.
Ordnance Survey maps: 1:50,000 sheet 186; 1:25,000 sheets SU84 and SU83.

A lovely walk on the extensive sandy heathlands bordering Frensham Little Pond and the Devil's Jumps, where there are magnificent views across to the Hog's Back and to Hampshire and Sussex. The walk continues over Kettlebury and Yagden Hills to Stockbridge Pond and Tilford. There are no stiles and very little mud and the stiffish climb up the Devil's Jump can be avoided if wished.

Bus: The 217 Alder Valley (Farnham-Grayshott, not Sundays) stops outside the post office in Rushmoor village. Cross the road from the garage to the bridleway opposite by the MOD sign and continue the walk at the paragraph marked (*).
Car park: There is a large car park at Frensham Little Pond situated on a minor road near the lake about a mile from the A287. From Hindhead take the first turning on the right after Frensham Great Pond.
Refreshments: There are inns at Tilford and Churt and a post office and general store in Rushmoor.

From the large car park at Frensham Little Pond, cross the grassy playing area to the road opposite the toilets and skirt the top of the lake on a path near the road. Turn half-right on a path by a National Trust sign and go through wooden barriers by the side of the lake, soon crossing over a stream in a hollow by some sluice gates. Keeping the lake on the right, continue along its banks for a few hundred yards and, where the path forks by some concrete posts at the corner of a field, still keep on the narrow path by the lake. On coming to the end of this part of the lake, continue on a path between wire fences with a field on the left. After nearly half a mile, pass through a metal barrier by a field where horses are kept, continue over a crossing track and almost immediately turn right down a dirt track just before a house.

At a minor road turn left for about 100 yards and by a house on the left cross the road to a bridleway opposite. Follow the path across the heathland towards the three peaks of the Devil's Jumps, soon coming to a beautiful secluded lake, fringed with rhododendrons and pines. Branch off on a path with the lake on the right, towards a pine grove, and continue round to just before the end of the lake. Fork left and, on reaching the main path once more, turn right to a junction of paths. Continue forward on a wide sandy path towards the highest of the three peaks. At a crossing track, one can avoid climbing the hill by turning left on a path, with two houses slightly to the right on the skyline, and cross the heath to join the walk shortly before the post office in Rushmoor. For the more energetic it is well worth the short steep climb for the magnificent views from the top towards the Hog's Back to the north and across to Hindhead to the south. At the crossing track take the second path on the left, soon climbing up the steep side of the hill by steps.

If you wish to visit the Pride of the Valley inn at Churt, cross the reddish stone crag at the summit and go down a path the other side which soon reaches a wire fence, turn left and at the corner of the fence turn right down to the road. Turn left for the inn and rejoin the walk by turning left at the road for about half a mile to the post office at Rushmoor. To avoid the road walking, turn left at the crag on the summit and take the sandy path down some wooden steps. At a fork keep right for a few yards and go to the right of small trees in a clearing, bear left and take a small path on the right with views to the left. At a wire fence turn left and follow the fence down past some houses until you come to a wide sandy track. At the end turn right between fences out to the road. Turn left over Sandy Lane to the post office and bus stop at Rushmoor.

(*)Cross the road from the garage to a path by a Ministry of Defence notice leading into Hankley Common. Soon go over a small stream up to a large clearing with telegraph wires. Cross the clearing to take the wide path uphill. Continue on this path, ignoring paths off to either side, until the path forks. Take the main, very sandy, path on the left and follow it uphill and then cross the shallow valley to the hill beyond. Bear right to the top of Kettlebury Hill and turn left on a broad track with fine views to the right. At a fork just past a pillbox, keep right. After nearly a mile on this fine ridge path, at a meeting of paths called the Lion's Mouth, bear left downhill towards wooden bars on a hill ahead. At the bottom of the slope, cross over a track and bear off to the left at the foot of the hillock towards the golf course. At the eleventh tee, turn right along a path by Yagden Hill. When this path divides into three, with fine views of Crooksbury Hill ahead, take the left-hand path going slightly downhill. Go over a crossing track and at a T junction turn left. At a wide clearing in the woods, take the path bearing off to the left and follow this down to a small car park near Stockbridge Pond. Go along the unmade track with the pond on the left until you reach the road.

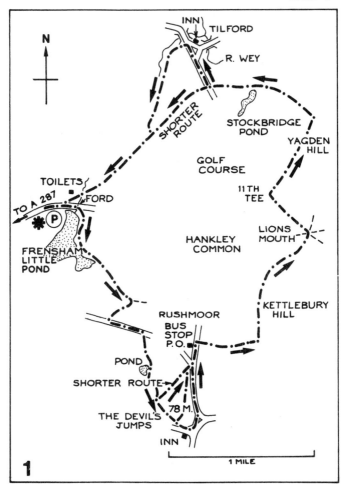

At this point one can take a short cut back to the car park at Frensham Little Pond or extend the walk slightly by visiting Tilford and returning via the river Wey.

For the shorter route, cross the road to a bridleway opposite and follow the path for about a mile and a half, keeping left at a fork, eventually passing the toilets to reach the road by the car park.

For the longer route, turn right along the road for about a quarter of a mile towards the green at Tilford. This large triangle of turf is famous for its cricket pitch and the ancient oak on the north side of the green, which is reckoned to be some nine hundred years old and is 10 feet (3.05 m) in diameter at its widest point. The Barley Mow inn was built in about 1700. The shallow water at the foot of the picturesque bridge is much favoured by canoeists and paddlers in the summer months. At the end of the cricket green, with the pub on the right and just before another bridge ahead, turn left to a public footpath through a small gate. Turn left for a few yards and take the footpath between hedges, passing the delightful Malt House on the right and the river Wey. Continue on the track between wire fences and go through a gate to enter a wood. Go over a crossing track and continue forward to join a track coming in from the left. At the end of some outbuildings, go forward on a path through the trees. This path eventually joins another track. Turn right and continue along the track for about half a mile to go over a water splash and past the toilets for the car park.

To return to the bus stop at Rushmoor, turn left on reaching the road, passing the end of the lake to continue the walk by taking the path by the National Trust sign mentioned in the first paragraph.

2. Puttenham Common, Waverley Abbey and Tilford

Distance: 11, 7½ or 4½ miles.
Grid references: 919461 (walks A and C); 910457 (walk B).
Ordnance Survey maps: 1:50,000 sheet 186; 1:25,000 sheets SU94 and SU84.

This walk of 11 miles can be split into two parts. Walk A from the upper car park at Puttenham Common is 4½ miles and crosses the common to the lakes and then returns via Cut Mill Pond and field paths to the car park. Walk B (7½ miles) starts from the lower car park near The Tarn and goes over Crooksbury Common to pass the ruins of Waverley Abbey on the far banks of the river Wey. It then passes through Tilford and returns to the car park by pleasant paths and bridleways. Walk C combines both walks.

Bus: The Alder Valley bus from Puttenham stops outside the upper car park at Puttenham Common and also the lower car park at the crossroads at Cut Mill.
Car parks: Walks A and C start from the large car park at

Puttenham Common. After the church in Puttenham village, turn left down Suffield Lane, signposted to Elstead and Cut Mill. After about 1½ miles turn right into the car park. The entrance is rather concealed and is on a fairly sharp right-hand bend. Walk B starts from the car park near the crossroads at Cut Mill about a mile further on. Turn right to the car park.

Refreshments: In Tilford, or the Donkey inn at Charleshill, in Walks B and C.

For Walks A and C

At the large car park at Puttenham Common, where there are fine views across to Crooksbury Hill and the wireless mast which is passed in Walks B and C, go across some sandy hillocks and turn right down steps into a shallow valley and straight up the path on the other side. Keep ahead over crossing tracks and then go downhill to a main crossing track. Turn left slightly downhill to a T junction. Turn right and fork left in 25 yards and immediately left again to go uphill to a viewpoint. Turn left with fine views on the left and keep on main track, eventually bending right to a wide sandy track. Turn left along this broad track to some woods by a fence. Turn left downhill, passing the large Hampton Park estate on the right and soon the rather muddy eighteenth century General's Pond on the left. Bear right and keep on the path to the large lakes called Warren Pond and The Tarn.

On reaching the causeway between the two lakes cross this and follow the path round the lake on the left, over the small footbridge. Where the path leaves the lake, follow it through the trees to a small car park near the road. Turn right for about 500 yards and at a bend, opposite a house on the right, cross the road to a divergence of paths. Walks A and C divide at this point.

For Walk A, take the cart track going slightly uphill with telegraph poles on the left, and follow this track past a new pumping station on the right for over half a mile to reach a minor road. Turn left for a few hundred yards to a definite crossing track. Turn right to cross the common out to a road. Bear slightly left and cross the road to the bridleway opposite to join Walk C again at the last paragraph.

For Walk B. At the car park, on the right of the crossroads coming from Puttenham and bordering the lake, continue up the road for about 500 yards to a bend, opposite a house on the right.

For Walks B and C. At the divergence of paths opposite the house, take the sandy track on the right between gateposts, and keep on this path, ignoring side turnings, passing pine woods on the left. Bear slightly left at a fork through a wood. On reaching the road, turn right and in about a quarter of a mile turn left at a bridlepath sign. This small path soon joins a wide track. Keep ahead under telegraph wires and just before a pine wood ahead,

9

branch left slightly uphill on a stony track. At a fork of sandy tracks with a notice saying 'Crooksbury Conservation Area', keep right and continue on this track for about half a mile to a T junction with another conservation notice. Turn right and after some way, after passing a house on the right and two houses on the left, turn off left on a wide path. On coming to a minor road ahead, turn left, soon passing the very tall wireless mast which was seen from the Puttenham Common car park. When the made-up road ends, continue on the track for nearly half a mile to a road.

Turn right along the road for 200 yards, and then turn left down a bridleway. After passing the delightful Crooksbury Cottage, this track leads down to a road where you turn right. In about 300 yards, at a right-hand bend, turn left down a sandy track. The river Wey is just visible through the trees down on the right and there is soon a vista across the water meadows to the ruins of Waverley Abbey. This Cistercian house was founded as early as 1128 and was the first Cistercian monastery in England. It was damaged by a serious flooding of the Wey in 1233. About 35 yards past a group of yews on the right, turn right on a small, pretty path through rhododendrons, which follows the river initially. After leaving the river and climbing up a small hill, the path divides and we take the left-hand fork. (For a closer look at the ruins across the river, take the right-hand fork and return the same way.) Keep on this path with fields on one side and a wood on the other and ignore a left turning after some way. On joining a small road, just after a notice saying 'Herons Wey Surrey West Girl Guides' with the Wey ahead, turn left and out to a road. Turn right towards a picturesque river bridge and almost immediately turn left on a path going uphill. After passing the beautiful Tilhill House on the left, branch off to the right, with the river down on the right. On reaching the road it is worth turning right over the much photographed bridge at Tilford to the beautiful cricket green and the Barley Mow Inn.

To continue the walk, retrace your steps over the bridge and go past the Post Office and Stores. After a few hundred yards, just before a sharp bend to the left, take the first small road to the right (Whitmead) and turn left by a grassy triangle to go immediately right on a drive. At the end of the drive, take the footpath on the right. This is a beautiful path with fine views to the right looking across to Hankley Common and beyond. Cross over two minor roads, keeping to the fence, and then cross a track to continue on the same footpath out to a road. Turn right and continue along the road until just past the Donkey inn on the right.

Cross the road and go up a track for a short way, then turn right up a sandy path with a bridleway sign. This soon joins a

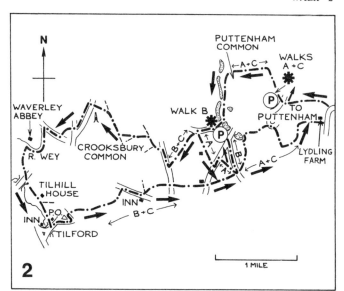

metalled drive by the entrance to a large estate. On reaching some tall wrought iron gates on the right, go left down the drive past the stone entrance pillars out to the road. Cross this to the bridleway opposite, which eventually leads out past Fulbrook Farm to a road. Cross the road to the cart track opposite, and after about 150 yards go through a small gate in the fence bordering a field, on the left. Cross the field diagonally right to a just visible gate. Go through the gate and continue down a small path, cross over a reddish stream and soon come out to a road. (For Walk B turn left and continue on this road to the car park by the crossroads.) Turn left and after a short distance, after a cottage on the right, pass a minor road and then immediately take the bridleway into the woods on the right.

For Walks A and C. Keep on this bridleway until reaching a brick track. Cross this towards Cutmill Pond and go over a small bridge with railings. Follow the path round by the edge of the attractive pond. Keep on past a flight of wooden steps down on the right to join the drive at the end of a grassy bank. Turn right and follow the drive with a hedge on the left and an old wall on the right. When the drive ends by Willow Cottage, take the path ahead between the wall and a garage, first crossing over some wooden planks. The path comes out on to a lane. Turn right

11

along this for a short way and, where the drive goes into a house, bear off slightly right to a public bridleway sign. At the next T junction turn left and continue on a wide and sandy track. At a junction turn left and follow this path for nearly a mile past Lydling Farm and out to a road. Turn left and at a bend to the right turn left and cross a stile. Cross another stile and keep to the right-hand hedge of a large field to a corner of a wood. Take the path along the right hand edge of the wood in the same direction. Cross a track to go ahead by a new plantation to a T junction. Turn right and after some way, in a deep gulley, turn left steeply uphill on a small path which soon passes a cottage and out to the road. The car park is opposite.

3. Normandy, Ash and Flexford

Distance: 6½ miles.
Grid reference: 927516.
Ordnance Survey maps: 1:50,000 sheet 186; 1:25,000 sheets SU95 and SU94.

This walk of about 6½ miles first crosses Normandy Common, then ventures on the wild heathland and pinewoods skirting the army ranges. After climbing Normandy Hill, with excellent views across the ranges and towards the Hog's Back, we descend towards Ash and continue on a very different terrain following farm lanes and footpaths across fields. This latter part of the walk can be muddy and boots are advisable.

Trains: From Ash station, join the walk by turning left and almost immediately right over a small footbridge by a 'No horses' sign. Cross a field planted with vegetables and at a minor road turn right to join the walk at (*).
Buses: Alder Valley, Guildford to Aldershot, stops in Normandy village near the food store. The car park is opposite.
Cars: Car park on right opposite food store on A323 at minor crossroads, just past Normandy village, if coming from Guildford.
Refreshments: Inns in Normandy and Ash.

Cross the footbridge on the left at the rear of the car park, pass some tennis courts and on to a football ground. Turn left on a track towards a cottage. Keep to the right of the cottage, and continue ahead over crossing tracks on a pleasant path which eventually emerges at a well kept cricket ground. Turn left and skirt the ground to about 15 yards before the pavilion. Turn left on initially a bracken-lined path heading NW, keeping left at a

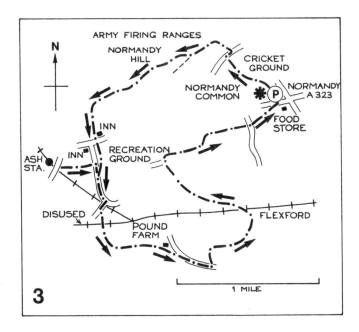

ARMY FIRING RANGES

N

NORMANDY
HILL

CRICKET
GROUND

NORMANDY
COMMON

NORMANDY
A 323

INN

FOOD
STORE

ASH
STA.

INN

RECREATION
GROUND

DISUSED

FLEXFORD

POUND
FARM

1 MILE

3

main fork and continue through young yews to reach a road. Cross over to a track marked by a notice warning you not to touch suspicious objects.

After 150 yards turn right at a house through a barred entrance. Follow the track to open heathland where the flagpoles denoting the danger areas are situated. If the red flags are flying the rattle of the guns should be evident by now. Do not venture near the flags but bear left on a wide track. Ignore a side turning on the left after 200 yards and continue on this track, which soon descends into a shallow depression. Keep on past wide right-hand turnings and then a crossing track, and at the next crossing path turn right towards Normandy Hill. Follow this narrow sandy path going up to the top of the hill. There are marvellous views here across to the Hog's Back and over the firing ranges.

The flat top of the hill is surrounded by a shallow ditch. At the gap in the western edge of the ditch and embankment, go half left (SW) for 70 yards to the edge of a steeply dropping path. Turn right, ignore the first small path and take the second path downhill with a tree-covered slope on the left. Ignore forks and turnings, and keep on the main path in a westerly direction for 500 yards.

This beautiful path eventually comes to a small fork; bear left and at a crossing track almost immediately keep forward on a track going downhill. On reaching a large Scots pine, turn right to reach a shallow pond. Keep the pond on the right and go forward south-west towards hillocks. Go over the hillocks with a wire fence on the left. At the corner of the wire fence, turn left past some houses down to a car park and out to a road. Cross this slightly right to an opening opposite. There are inns on both sides of the road here. Cross the recreation ground to a small road on the right by some cottages. Turn to the left.

(*)Keep on this minor road for about a quarter of a mile and go right over the railway bridge. Soon turn left at a public footpath sign opposite a cottage. The path can be muddy but soon improves and becomes a cinder track. At a road turn left over a bridge across a disused railway track. Turn off left at a footpath sign through woods on a rather wet path, but drier alternatives can be found. At a line of bungalows turn left down a wide green avenue lined with trees.

After passing Pound Farm and a duckpond turn right on to a metalled road. Continue past some houses and a farm until the road degenerates into a cart track. After about 150 yards turn left down a footpath. After some way this path bends sharply right and continues downhill through woods eventually coming to a metalled lane leading past some bungalows on the outskirts of Flexford. Just before a railway embankment, turn left by a footpath sign and follow the path between wire fences, crossing two stiles and then over the railway line. Go down through a copse and over a very tall stile out to a field. Cross the field diagonally left, over a drainage ditch in the centre and on to a path leading to a gap in the hedges by a solitary tree. Cross the next field to the far right hand corner, over a stile and out to a track on the right. Keep forward (NW) to eventually pass under some pylons. Ignore a turning on the right and a road to a house on the left, and take the next right turning leading into a field. Turn sharp right at a low bank to the edge of a wood then left along the wood to a stile. Bear diagonally left across a field to a stile and cross this to go forward to the left-hand edge of a sports field. Continue down to a line of houses. Cross a stile and go down a passage to the road. Turn right and cross the road to a footpath. Follow the clear path diagonally left across a field to reach the main road after passing the backs of some houses. Turn right to the car park. (For Ash station, continue from the first paragraph.)

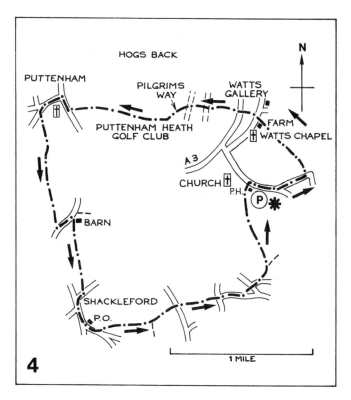

4. Compton, Puttenham and Shackleford

Distance: 7½ miles.
Grid reference: 956470.
Ordnance Survey maps: 1:50,000 sheet 186; 1:25,000 sheet SU94.

This walk encompasses the attractive villages of Compton, Puttenham and Shackleford and is chiefly along field paths and the Pilgrims' Way. The tenth-century church at Compton with its unique two-storeyed chancel is well worth a visit and we go near the Watts Gallery, which contains a large number of the artist's paintings. There is not too much mud and no steep hills.

15

Buses: 260, Guildford - Compton - Godalming (not Sundays).
Car park: From the Godalming bypass (A3) turn down to Compton. Park in layby outside the village hall, near the Harrow public house.
Refreshments: Inns in each of the three villages and general stores in Shackleford.

From the parking spot turn left if you wish to visit the church. To start the walk turn right and take the third turning on the left, Polsted Lane, which is on the far side of an open space used as playing fields. After about a quarter of a mile, just before a 'No through road' sign, take the footpath on the left through a wooden gate. After nearly half a mile cross a stile and make for a stile in the right-hand corner of the field. Turn right along the path between fences to a stile ahead and turn left. The tall building in red brick, looking rather like a Greek Orthodox chapel, standing on a hillock on the left, is a memorial chapel to the artist G. F. Watts and was erected by the artist's wife in 1896. There is a water tower on the skyline on the left which is seen later in the walk from the opposite direction.

Just before some farm sheds turn right into woods and immediately left on a path through the trees which runs parallel to the farm. Cross a stile to reach a minor road. The memorial chapel is to the left and the Watts Gallery is on the right a short distance down the road and the times of opening can be seen outside. Cross the road to a wide cart track opposite, marked North Downs Way, and continue under two bridges. Fork left immediately and keep ahead. At a junction follow the North Downs Way sign once more (second right) and soon the path crosses the beautiful Puttenham Heath golf course. This path eventually merges with a small metalled road which leads out to Hook Lane opposite the Jolly Farmer inn.

Keep on the North Downs Way by turning right and then left towards Puttenham. This is an attractive village with many beautiful old houses and cottages. After passing the church, turn left down Suffield Lane and at the end of the wall continue forward following the footpath sign across some pleasantly undulating fields, keeping a wire fence on the left. At the end of the field there is a fine view looking back towards the church, priory and Hog's Back, an ancient trackway of pre-Roman times. Ignore the gate to a field and take the stile ahead near a stone folly, continue over two more stiles and follow the straight path ahead by a wire fence. Here you will see the water tower again on the left. At the end of the fence go round the edge of a field to a stile in the fence and go straight across the next field to a copse and continue down a dip to a stile ahead. Follow the fence past a water trough to the end of the field and over a stile on to a road.

Turn left and carry on up the road to an old barn standing in some fields on the right. Turn right on to a public footpath, passing the barn on the left. At a gate marked private, turn right over a stile and diagonally left to another stile. Continue in the same direction across the field, aiming for the left of a low farm building, and then keep to the left of two big trees in the next field and on to the right hand corner where there is a rather obscure path leading out to a road. Turn right to The Street at Shackleford. Turn left through the village, past a turning to Cut Mill on the right, to a fork by a post office. Bear left up Grenville Road for a short distance and then leave the road in favour of Rokers Lane on the left. Keep on this track for about half a mile, ignoring a turn-off to the right. Cross a main road to take the track ahead with storage sheds on the right. Follow the path through the large market garden to a road and continue in the same direction up the road ahead. Turn left on a marked footpath by a telephone pole. At the end of this short path, cross the road and take the small residential road opposite. After passing Broomfield Manor, go down a narrow downhill path on the right of a gatepost to a house.

At the field at the bottom of the path turn left through the swing gate and follow the path between fences and hedges out to a cart track. Continue uphill and before the white manor house on the right, climb over a stile on the left and cross the field diagonally right to the edge of a copse. Go over a stile and continue on with a fence on the left. Cross three further stiles past the farmyard and go down a narrow path between fences, over a concrete stile and out to the road by the side of the Harrow public house.

5. Winkworth Arboretum, Hydons Ball and Hascombe

Distance: 9, 7 or 6 miles.
Grid references: 989412 (main car park), 997415 (lower car park).
Ordnance Survey maps: 1:50,000 sheet 186; 1:25,000 sheets SU94, SU93 and TQ03.

This is a lovely walk starting from Winkworth Arboretum near Godalming, with its fine displays of azaleas and rhododendrons in spring and glorious autumnal colouring. From the arboretum the walk crosses Juniper Valley and Hydons Heath to climb Hydons Ball and then over Hydons Heath to Hascombe village. The longer walk encircles Hascombe Hill with its iron age encampment and fine views across the Weald to the South Downs.

Car: There are two car parks in the arboretum – the lower car park is reached from Guildford by turning right in Bramley village off the A281 on a minor road for about 2 miles. This gives the opportunity of walking through the arboretum and adds about half a mile to the walk in both directions. The main car park is off the B1230, about 2 miles south of Godalming.

Refreshments: There is a National Trust refreshment chalet in the arboretum, open from April to end October except Mondays (open Bank Holiday Mondays and some weekends and fine days in March). There is also an inn in Hascombe village.

From the lower car park at the arboretum, go through the gate by the sign that gives times of opening for refreshments. At another gate just before the lake turn right on a path bordering the end of the lake and go up the steps between the azaleas. Turn right at a crossing track and continue on past the toilets and refreshment hut to the main car park.

From the main car park, keep to the left of the parking area and go through a gap in the fence to cross the road to a lane opposite, marked 'South Munstead Lane and Farm'. When the lane bends to the right, bear left by a South Munstead farm sign. At the driveway to a cottage ahead, go down a narrow stony path, ignoring side paths marked 'Private'. Continue on through pinewoods and down to a T junction. Turn left and after a few yards fork left to go through a small gate and immediately take the right-hand path going uphill with a field down to the left. Ignore side turnings and bear right at a T junction. On emerging at a lane, cross to a path opposite and keep on ahead on the main track to reach a junction of paths. Bear right with a pond on the left. Just before an enormous beech tree turn right up a narrow path to a wide sandy track. Here you have the choice either to climb Hydons Ball or to take a short cut round the bottom of the hill.

To climb Hydons Ball, turn right and in about 50 yards turn left and then take the right fork uphill, ignoring small crossing tracks. This path leads up to the Hydons Ball trig point with its underground water tanks marked by manhole covers. The view is somewhat marred by the pines that have been planted too close to the top but there are glimpses of the magnificent panorama of the South Downs. There is also a seat dedicated to Octavia Hill, one of the founders of the National Trust. Keep across the clearing in the same direction, passing close by the manhole cover beyond the trig point, and take the path ahead leading downhill. Ignore a left turn and at a T junction with a fence ahead turn left downhill passing a memorial stone on the right. At the bottom of the hill continue forward with the pumping station on the right.

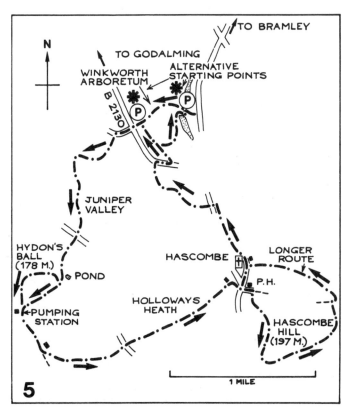

5

1 MILE

For those who did not climb the hill, turn left at the crossing track and continue down to where the track descends from the hill. Turn left past the pumping station and both walks continue together. Continue along this track and after passing a public bridleway on the left turn left on to a narrow public bridleway which climbs up above the track. Keep on this pretty path, which weaves through the trees with an occasional glimpse of lovely views on the right. Shortly after leaving the edge of a field, at a fork where the path goes downhill, bear left. Keep on this small, rather brambly path winding through the wood until it enters a field. Keep on in the same direction with a barbed-wire fence on the right. Chinthurst tower can be seen in the distance on the left. Go through the gate and along the edge of the next field to

19

enter the wood. Wild deer can sometimes be seen here. At the end of the wood cross the minor road to a path opposite and continue forward when a path comes in on the right. Keep on this path up the valley across Holloways Heath through once beautiful larch and silver birch woods devastated by the hurricane in October 1987.

The path, after about a mile, leads down into the valley past an old house on the left. At a pond bear right and go through a gate to cross a field to the inn ahead at Hascombe village.

For the longer walk (9 miles), at the White Horse inn go up the drive to the right of the inn, turn right by a house and go to the right of a wooden garage to take a sunken footpath. At a junction of paths bear left and continue uphill when another track comes in on the right and into a wood with rhododendrons. At the top of a rise bear off right past large beech trees to follow the main path running round the escarpment of Hascombe Hill with wonderful views across to the Sussex Downs (again the fallen trees are much in evidence here but the views are greatly improved). Keep on this path round the hill and when the track forks ahead, take the left fork going slightly uphill. Bear left by a fence to a field, and at the bottom of the hill there is a fine rural view to the left looking down the valley to the hills in the distance. Turn right up a sunken track and in 60 yards turn left through an avenue of trees with a field to the left and a view of Hascombe Church. Bear left at the end of the avenue and on coming to a fork go left between wooden gateposts. Continue on this broad sandy track, ignoring side turnings, for about three quarters of a mile. Later the path leads behind some houses to join a lane just before a picturesque pond with seats with Hascombe Church ahead. Bear right, before the pond, past the noisy geese and hens.

If you do not wish to go round Hascombe Hill, turn down the 'no through road' to the left of the inn, go past the village pond and bear left past the geese and hens.

Both walks continue together. Just before a house facing you on the left, turn off the metalled road to a path on the left and at a fork keep on the path to reach a stony track. Continue forward past some stables and go through a gate and on to another metal gate ahead. Turn left on a path between fields to cross a road to a small drive opposite by a house. At the end of the drive, keep on up the hill on a deeply indented path. After passing a fine manor house at the top turn left by a brick wall on to a metalled road. Turn right at the junction up to the main road. Turn right along the road towards two houses on the left. Take the small path between the houses and continue along this enclosed path. For the lower car park turn right into the arboretum. For refreshments and the main car park continue on this path.

6. Chilworth, Shalford and the Chantries

Distance: 5½ miles (7 miles from Chilworth station).
Grid reference: 024473.
Ordnance Survey maps: 1:50,000 sheet 186; 1:25,000 sheets TQ04 and SU94.

A very varied walk through farmland to Shalford and on to the water meadows and towpath of the river Wey leading to Guildford. The return journey is made along the Chantries with fine views across to Hascombe Hill. Very little mud will be encountered.

Trains: Chilworth and Albury station. Turn left from the station along the A248, Dorking Road, and take the first turning on the right, Blacksmith Lane.
Buses: 425, 439, 450 (Monday to Saturday). Bus stop in A248 by Blacksmith Lane.
Car parks: After passing Chilworth station (if coming from Albury) turn right down Blacksmith Lane and park in side road, or there is a small car park off Pilgrim's Way below the Chantries (start the walk from A).
Refreshments: Inns at Shalford and Guildford.

At the sharp bend to the right where Blacksmith Lane joins Halfpenny Lane, take the signposted footpath across the road which goes uphill between fences. After a short time you will see Chilworth Manor on the right through the trees. This house has origins going back to Saxon times and was once owned by Sarah, widow of the great Duke of Marlborough. When the path emerges on to Halfpenny Lane once more, turn left and almost immediately take the path across the fields by the letter box. After nearly a mile the track reaches a farm; climb the stile in the hedge on the right and bear left, i.e. continue in a forward direction. There is a fine view of the ruins of St Catherine's Priory on a little knoll ahead, on the other side of the Wey, which is passed later in the walk. Also on this stretch you can see Guildford Cathedral on the right and the copper spire of Shalford Church.

At a small residential road turn left on to a small footpath running parallel to the road. Cross a road to some steps opposite and a stile and continue forward alongside a barbed-wire fence through a field of horses, over the Tillingbourne to the fine eighteenth-century watermill at Shalford. This was a working corn mill until 1914 and is sometimes open to the public. Keep forward past the mill out on to the main road with the Sea Horse public house opposite. This is the village of Shalford and the church is a short distance along the road to the right. This was rebuilt in 1846 and the pulpit is carved with ships and a shield as a memorial to a young sailor who was lost with his ship in the First World War. By the church is Shalford House, dating back to Tudor times though externally late eighteenth-century; it belonged to the Austen family for three hundred years.

Turn right from the mill and cross the road to a footpath by the side of the Sea Horse car park. When this track bends to the left carry on for a few yards to a five-barred gate and turn left alongside a wire fence with views over the water meadows. When this path ends, cross the stile on the right and go downhill to the river Wey. Follow the path, keeping the river on the right, and cross a small footbridge at the weir, past a cottage on the right and continue along the towpath to the lock. Cross two bridges to the far towpath and follow the path along to Guildford. This is a very pleasant path with plenty of interest along the route. In the summer pleasure boats take visitors from Guildford to Godalming and near the footbridge there is a small grotto on the left marking the site where the pilgrims crossed the river. If you wish to visit the ruins of St Catherine's Priory continue up the small road by the grotto and you will see the ruins at the top of the hill on the left.

(A short cut can be taken across the footbridge which links the Pilgrim's Way. On the other side of the river turn left to the post and follow the main path round to the right. Keep ahead and eventually cross a playing field to the main road. Cross to Pilgrim's Way opposite.)

For the longer walk, continue to the end of the towpath, and cross the footbridge on to the main road. Guildford town is away to the left as is the Yvonne Arnaud Theatre, which was built by public subscription and opened in 1965. Take a path to the right of the road leading past the rowing club. Follow this past the sports pavilion to where the road called the Pilgrim's Way is on the left. This is where the short cut joins the main route.

Go down Pilgrim's Way and pass two roads on the right. Turn right down a lane signposted North Downs Way and pass a small car park.

(**A**) At the white cottage at the end of the lane go through a gate on the right and keep left up the hill through the Chantries for about half a mile. At the top, where there is a large clearing with some seats, keep ahead on the same path for about 50 yards. By a red pole marked '7', bear right along the path to eventually reach the open down. Turn left and walk along the top of the open downs with marvellous views across to Hascombe Hill and beyond on the right. Pass through a gap in the hedge

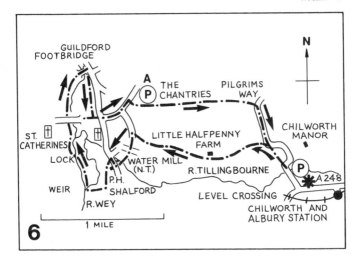

and go forward through a gap in the trees in the same direction. Here one can see the small church of St Martha's ahead in its commanding position on top of the hill.

Towards the end of the open downs, drop down to a lower parallel path to go through a gap in the trees, then with a fenced field on the left. Cross a stile on the left and turn right along the side of the field to the concealed entrance to a path in the corner. Follow the path steeply downhill through woods and turn right at the T junction at the bottom out to a lane. Turn right again and at the corner by the 'No horses' sign those starting the walk from the Chantries should turn right and take the path through the fields by the letter box (mentioned in the first paragraph). To reach Halfpenny Lane go down the path on the right between hedges. Continue down Blacksmith Lane for the main road and the station and buses.

7. Ripley, the Wey Navigation and Pyrford and Old Woking

Distance: 8 or 5 miles.
Grid reference: 053569.
Ordnance Survey maps: 1:50,000 sheets 186 and 187; 1:25,000 sheet TQ05.

A walk along the banks of the Wey Navigation canal and the river Wey with an extension to Old Woking. There are no hills and very few stiles.

Bus: The Green Line bus 715 (Guildford-Kingston-Oxford Circus, hourly weekdays and two-hourly Sundays) stops outside the post office in Ripley village. Cross the road from the post office if coming from Kingston and turn right down a small road between the Craft Centre and a paper shop, cross Ripley Green diagonally right and join the walk from the car park at the cricket pitch.

Car park: There is a small car park behind the shops in the centre of Ripley village, on the right-hand side if coming from Esher, or, if this is full, you can park on the green facing the cricket pitch.

Refreshments: At Ripley or the Anchor Inn on the Wey Navigation canal and in Old Woking.

Ripley was once a coaching village and there are still many inns and half-timbered houses dating from Tudor and Elizabethan times. The broad main street has greatly benefited from the opening of the bypass and there are still some signs that it was a gathering point for the London cyclists. The village green has been the scene of cricket matches since the eighteenth century.

From the car park take the wide track across the green with the cricket pitch on the right. You will soon see a large house, Dunsborough Park, on the left, the gardens of which are sometimes open to the public. At the end of some farm cottages, where the track ahead is marked 'Strictly private', bear left on a path which soon crosses the Ockham Mill stream and then at a house go slightly left between holly bushes and over a footbridge and continue to the lock and weir. You may be lucky enough to see herons on this stretch of water meadow.

Cross over the weir and turn right past the lock cottage. Do not go over the small footbridge but continue along the towpath, which lies between the Wey Navigation canal and river Wey for a short distance. The Wey Navigation canal was planned three hundred years ago by Sir Richard Weston of Sutton Place and runs between Weybridge and Guildford. The original bridges and locks were built from the ruins of Oatlands Palace in Weybridge.

Keep on the towpath for about a mile past many attractively decorated barges and houseboats until the lock and the Anchor public house are reached. Turn left across the bridge, passing a notice about the footpath being moved 200 yards, continue along the road and turn left through a farm gate across a well-kept field of vegetables. Turn right on a track and bear left past a small greenhouse to emerge on to a road. Turn left and after a short distance turn right down Elveden Close. At the end of this road

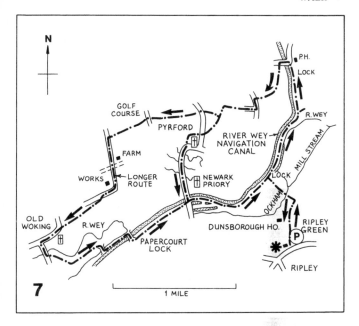

take a footpath over a stile to the right of a house.

Turn left at the end of the footpath and continue on a track between fields to cross a stile. For the shorter walk continue from the paragraph marked (A).

For the longer walk turn right over another stile up the side of a field. At the top of the field look back for some fine views over to the Surrey Hills. Turn right over the stile and on out to a road. Cross to the bridleway opposite and follow this for nearly a mile to eventually cross a golf course. At a small road turn left to Roundbridge farm and pass this on the right to continue ahead along a small road. After the sewage works turn right and at some houses turn left on a small path between garages. Cross the ditch and turn right along a field path to eventually cross a stile into a wood and out to the main road at a corner. Turn left through Old Woking passing Church Street with the old church. At a roundabout turn left and at the end of houses turn left into fields. Keep on a cart track ahead with the river winding away on the left. Go through a gate to reach a stile by the river. Do not cross the stile but bear off right along grassy track to a bridge. Cross this bridge and turn left along the Wey Navigation canal.

Cross the canal at Papercourt lock, where the river joins the canal, and follow the towpath in the same direction to a road. Turn left over the bridge and right down the towpath. The two walks continue together from here. Continue from paragraph (B).

Shorter walk

(A) Continue on the track to cross a farmyard and emerge on a road. Turn left up to St Nicholas's church, Pyrford, which is set on a low knoll overlooking the ruins of Newark Priory. The church is Norman, complete and virtually unspoilt, with a Tudor porch. The interior has a marvellous timbered roof, the pews are fifteenth-century and the pulpit Jacobean. Opposite the nave is a wall painting dating from 1140. Go through the churchyard with the church on the left, down the gravel path and out on to the road once more. After about a quarter of a mile, passing on the left the ruins of Newark Priory, founded in the middle of the twelfth century, walk to the traffic lights and turn left down the towpath.

The two walks continue together

(B) The watermill that used to be here was burned to the ground in 1966. The site of a prehistoric village of about 1500 BC was discovered near Pyrford Lock in 1926. Cross the canal at the lock and continue along the towpath, the haunt of many fishermen. On reaching the lock and weir again, turn right and retrace the last half mile back to the car park at Ripley or to the buses.

8. Wisley Common and Ockham Common

Distance: 8 or 4 miles.
Grid reference: 068582.
Ordnance Survey maps: 1:50,000 sheet 187; 1:25,000 sheet TQ05.

A walk through the pinewoods of Wisley and Ockham commons, visiting the semaphore tower at Chatley Heath, which was last used to relay messages to the fleet at Portsmouth in 1848. The shorter walk goes on to skirt the large lake of Bolder Mere whilst the longer walk goes across fields and through woods past the villages of Martyrs Green and Ockham before crossing the A3 to Ockham Mill and the river Wey, finally traversing a small section of the Royal Horticultural Gardens at Wisley back to the car park.

Trains: The nearest station is at Effingham Junction, which is about a mile from point A on the longer walk, adding two miles to that walk. Turn left from the station and at the road junction turn right and immediately left. After nearly a mile, turn left at the second bridlepath, just before the hamlet of Mays Green.

Bus: The Green Line bus 715 (Oxford Circus to Guildford) and 740 (Victoria to Guildford) stop outside the Wisley Gardens turning on the A3. Walk up the road towards Wisley Gardens and at the fork just before the gardens keep right for about 70 yards to a small clearing on the right.

Car park: Take the RHS Wisley Gardens turning off the A3 (if approaching from Esher, continue past the turning to the next junction and cross under the bypass to return to Wisley Gardens). Shortly after turning down towards Wisley Gardens, take the right-hand fork and after about 70 yards turn off the road into a small clearing on the right. There is a large car park for the gardens down the fork on the left where there is a shop and garden centre and light refreshments are available. See also the map for car parks on either side of the A3.

Refreshments: On the longer walk, there are the Black Swan public house at Martyrs Green and the village Post Office and Stores at Ockham.

The walk starts by taking the main track marked by a single post at the rear of the clearing, just left of centre. Continue down this track, crossing a small stream, until you come to a large junction of paths. Take the second wide track on the left and after about 200 yards bear off to the right on the sandy path. In another 50 yards, turn left between silver birches and cross a stream almost immediately. Continue on this track for about half a mile soon with fields on the right. Wisley Common was once mined for iron and is still covered in parallel trenches. Near the main road is a tree-covered barrow at Cock Crow Hill, which was opened in the early twentieth century and showed signs of a cremation thousands of years old.

With the motorway ahead, bear round to the right with the track, and right again to pass some camping grounds. Continue on this track past a house on the right and a pond on the left. Take the track on the left opposite a posted horseride and cross the car park area ahead to a new footbridge over the A3.

Continue forward in the same direction for about 200 yards, and when a wide track soon runs parallel on the left, take a short path (marked N ↑) through the trees to join it and turn right towards a very large clearing with heather in the centre, bounded by posts.

With the clearing on the right, bear slightly left past seats until you come to a wide sandy track, marked by a line of posts, about halfway round (opposite a path across the centre). Turn left up this wide track and when the track bends to the left, go forward at post 4 up a smaller switchback path until you reach the top of

Telegraph Hill and the Chatley Heath semaphore tower. In the early nineteenth century the Admiralty used a line of thirteen similar hilltop semaphore stations to send messages to Portsmouth, a distance of 68 miles, in 15 minutes. There is a large post on the top with jointed arms which were used to send the messages. The tower is now open to the public in the summer at weekends and on Wednesdays.

Continue past the tower and go down the tarmac drive. At a left-hand bend keep ahead on a path for 60 yards and then turn right on a small path which passes several fine redwood trees. On reaching a shingle bridle track, the walks divide.

For the shorter walk (4 miles)

Turn right along the shingle track and at a junction take the second path on the left, between barriers ahead with a Chatley Heath sign. Follow the signs on the posts to reach a car park. Take the path at the rear of the car park (marked with a post) and follow the signs to turn left about 100 yards before another car park ahead, to cross the road to a path leading to a picnic spot by Boldermere Lake. This was once a hammer pond, which provided the water power to drive the heavy hammers in local iron works.

To continue the walk take a path about 100 yards away from the Mere circling the lake to the right, soon on a guided path which crosses the bog on planks. At a post bear right and at a second planked bridge fork right over more planks. Just before a fourth set of planks with a waymark ahead, turn left away from the lake, initially with grass on the left, to reach a lane.

A short extension across the old Wisley airfield can be taken here if wished. Cross the lane to a gate and bridleway which leads out to the wide open space of the airfield. Follow the path across the field and cross the runway to continue ahead to just before some farm buildings. Turn right over stile and go diagonally across a field to a footpath sign on the runway. Turn right between barriers towards houses and cross the field to tarmac. Turn left and follow the tarmac around to a gate out to a road and straight ahead to cross the A3 to the bus stop, or on to where the car is parked.

If you do not wish to take the extension, turn right along the lane to skirt the airfield to the entrance. Turn right to cross the A3.

For the longer walk (8 miles)

At the bridlepath turn left and then right at the next fork, coming out on to a lane with some cottages and a farm on the right. Bear left down the lane for about half a mile, passing Hatchford School on the left. When the lane gives way to a small road, turn left past Flower Cottage. (The Black Swan public house is a short way down the road to the right.) After passing

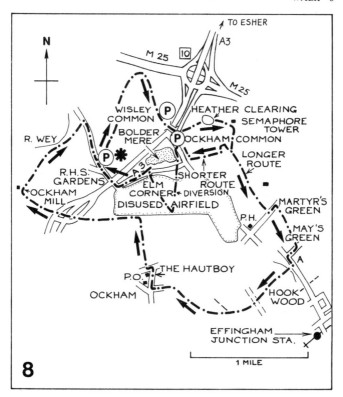

8

Flower Cottage in the small village of Martyrs Green, cross the road and mount some steps to reach an enclosed path through a kissing gate which leads to a cat hotel on the left. Continue forward on a tarmac drive with fine views ahead and to the left. When the drive swings to the left, keep forward across a field to a footpath sign and follow a path with a fence on the right. Soon cross a private garden out to a road over a stile. This is the hamlet of Mays Green. Turn right and at the main road turn left. After about 200 yards cross the road to a bridleway on the right.

(A) Those coming from the station join the walk here. Keep to the main bridleway, soon crossing a brick bridge and bearing to the right. This path crosses a grassy ride and eventually emerges at the corner of a field. Continue forward with a ditch on the right and fence on left and on reaching a concrete path, keep on in the same direction past some cottages on the right to a footpath sign by a gate. Go ahead through a second gate and after 70 yards turn right on a grassy crossing track marked 'PF No Horses'. At a T junction turn right to a gate and turn left by footpath sign. Go through a wood to emerge at a field with a stile. Cross the stile and bear diagonally right across the field to go through an opening and on in the same direction to a cart track. Continue past some fairly new houses on the right and then some delightful old cottages to reach a road, with Ockham post office on the corner opposite.

Turn right along the road, signposted Cobham, to the Hautboy restaurant on the corner. Turn left past the Hautboy and after a few yards cross the road to the footpath opposite. Go past the farm and up the track, eventually reaching a field. Continue forward to reach a stile and cross the valley to a bridleway. Turn left along the bridleway and at signed posts turn left along the edge of a field. Continue along in the same direction, keeping a wire fence on the left until the bypass comes into view. After passing a derelict cowshed on the left, go over a stile and continue forward to the slip road to the bypass. Turn left and cross the road. Go under the bypass via the footpath. Turn right and cross the road to the small road called Mill Lane.

Just before Ockham Mill (which is worth going to see) at the end of the lane, turn right by a footpath sign and continue past some bungalows and on across the large field. Cross a stile in the hedge and over another field to a stile leading to a path which first skirts Wisley Gardens and then goes through a lovely corner of the gardens with some fine specimen trees and the river Wey on the left. The Royal Horticultural Gardens at Wisley were established in 1904 and the grounds cover some 200 acres (81 ha) of land. At the end of the path, cross the stile and a service road and turn right down the minor road back to the clearing on the left and out to the main road for the bus. For the station turn into the clearing just before the fork to the gardens and continue from the first paragraph.

9. Holmbury St Mary, Ewhurst and Peaslake

Distance: 7½ miles.
Grid reference: 104451.
Ordnance Survey maps: 1:50,000 sheet 187; 1:25,000 sheets TQ14 and TQ04.

This walk has fine viewpoints from Holmbury and Pitch Hills and the picturesque villages of Ewhurst and Peaslake are visited. Some of the footpaths and bridleways are likely to be muddy in wet weather. There is a steep descent from Holmbury Hill.

Bus: The Alder Valley 201, 273 (Guildford via Cranleigh to Ewhurst), no Sunday service, stops by the village green in Ewhurst. Also the Tillingbourne 25, Cranleigh and Guildford. Start the walk from the paragraph marked (*).
Car: There is a small car park outside the youth hostel at Holmbury St Mary. Turn off the A25 on to the B2126 and just before the village of Holmbury St Mary take a small turning on the right signposted Radnor Lane and Woodhouse Lane (also marked with a Forestry Commission sign and YHA sign). Keep on this narrow lane until it peters out at Hurtwood Common.
Refreshments: Inns and general shops at Ewhurst and Peaslake.

Just beyond the car park outside Holmbury St Mary youth hostel, take the path to the right of the larger of the two notices saying 'Hurtwood Control'. On reaching a wide sandy track turn left and keep on this track for over half a mile and cross a wide track. After passing a small crossing track branch off left on a wide grassy path. Go over two crossing tracks and at a fork bear left on a sandy track. Keep ahead when a track comes in from the right. This path leads out to Holmbury Hill with its memorial stone seat and magnificent panorama across to the South Downs. Holmbury Hill is the site of a large iron age fortress and the two ditches, which once had a stockade between them, can still be seen surrounding all but the steep south-facing slope.

With your back to the memorial seat, walk south to take a narrow, very steep path which is the right hand one of two. This path has suffered from the effects of the October 1987 hurricane as a lot of the trees have been swept away. (An easier alternative can be found to the right of the path which comes out about 50 yards to the right of the main path.) At the end of the slope, the main path emerges at a road with a cottage on the right. Turn right past this delightful cottage and its neighbours and at the end of a brick wall on the left cross the drive and take a small path between hedges on the right-hand edge of a grassy area. This enclosed path leads down to some wooden steps out to a road, where you turn left and then immediately right on a track. Just past the house, by the pond, ranch off to the left along a sometimes muddy track. Go over a stile on the left to enter a field. Cross this field to a gate at the bottom and cross the next field half right to a stile just to one side of a tree with farm buildings in the distance behind it. Cross this next stile and continue in single file (if crops are growing) slightly left to yet another stile. Go across the fourth field to a stile and over a concrete bridge and continue forward again with trees and a ditch on the left. Enter a copse over a stile and soon cross a farm track. Continue forward with a field on the right. Follow the yellow waymarks over stiles and go along beside a field with iron railings on the right. At the end of the field go over another stile and follow the path through the wood. At the road turn left to the beautiful village green at Ewhurst, with an inn, the Boar's Head, on the left. The old but much restored church at Ewhurst is a short way down the road from the green.

(*) From the inn, cross the village green and go down a small road by the side of the garage. Ignore a turning off on the left, and after about half a mile, just after crossing a bridge over a stream, turn right on a footpath over a stile. Cross another stile and follow the path which crosses a ditch into a field. Go through a gate and turn left down the road, and in 40 yards turn right at the first turning. When the metalled track sweeps round to enter a private forecourt, go ahead on the bridleway through the trees. After houses on the right, turn sharply right through white metal posts to reach the road. Cross to the road opposite and go up this road to a house on the right called Follyhill.

At the fork here take the left-hand, unmade-up track going uphill. Follow this track for about three quarters of a mile, eventually coming to the ridge of Pitch Hill, where there are good views on the right since the trees have been cut down. When the broad track bears off to the left, turn sharply right on a small path leading towards a gate into a wood. Do not enter the wood, but turn left to follow the path downhill with the wood and fence on the right. This path leads out to a grassy verge by a house on the right. Follow the stony path out to the road and turn left for about half a mile to the village of Peaslake.

Just before the cross in the village, turn right for a few yards up Radnor Road and then turn left by a garage to a house, up a steep path. Cross a road and keep ahead up a tarmac lane which soon becomes a fenced track through trees. At the top, on reaching wooded common land, continue forward downhill. Cross a shallow valley and up the other side on a sunken path and then fields on the left. Go over crossing tracks in another shallow valley and continue forward when a path comes in on the left. Keep on the main sunken path and, after going down into a clearing, still keep on the main path going uphill. Go over a crossing track and maintain the same direction back to the car park by Holmbury St Mary youth hostel.

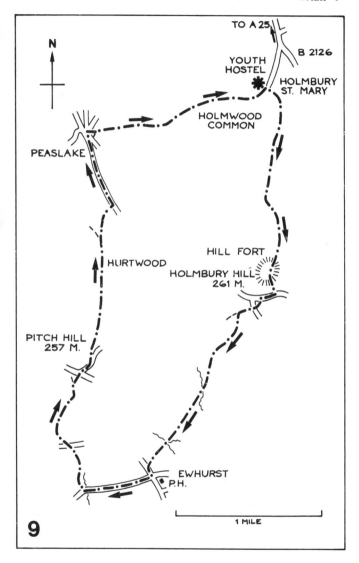

N

TO A25

B 2126

YOUTH HOSTEL

HOLMBURY ST. MARY

HOLMWOOD COMMON

PEASLAKE

HILL FORT

HURTWOOD

HOLMBURY HILL 261 M.

PITCH HILL 257 M.

EWHURST P.H.

1 MILE

9

10. Great Bookham Common and Effingham Common

Distance: 7½ or 4 miles.
Grid reference: 130557.
Ordnance Survey maps: 1:50,000 sheet 187; 1:25,000 sheets TQ15 and TQ05.

A walk over Great and Little Bookham commons, which comprise over 400 acres (162 ha) of oak and holly owned by the National Trust. The walk continues through woods and fields and there are plenty of blackberries to be picked in season along the hedgerows. The bridlepaths on the commons will be muddy after rain.

Trains: From Bookham station turn left towards the sharp bend in the road. The walk starts from the car park at Commonside on the left.
Bus: The bus stops outside Bookham station.
Car park: Turn off the A246 towards Great Bookham and continue on to the station. The car park is at Commonside, which is on a sharp bend just before the station.
Refreshments: In Great Bookham.

Take the main track at the far end of the car park and pass a railway bridge on the right. At the end of a field on the right, before some houses, take a parallel, sandy track on the left. At a T junction turn left. Keep on this main path for about half a mile, passing several ponds on the left. At a stony track with a house opposite turn right and continue past a bungalow with a National Trust sign. After a few yards at a junction of paths take the second on the left with a public bridleway sign. At the next signpost continue ahead (W). Cross over a small tributary of the Mole and continue past two houses on the left. After crossing another tributary, ignore the immediate turning on the right to a house and take the next turning on the right up a grassy track a short way to a stile leading into a large field. The walks divide at this point.

For the longer walk (7½ miles)
Cross the large field past two trees in the centre and make for a stile, just to the right of the two trees. Cross a bridge and a two-barred fence. The line of the path is now across the middle of the next field to a stile opposite. On the other side of this stile turn right and follow the hedge bounding the field towards a railway arch in the distance.

34

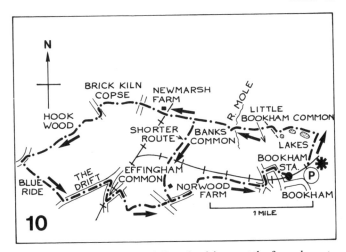

Go through the arch and follow the drive past the farm down to the road. Cross this to the footpath sign opposite. The path through the wood is rather overgrown. After some way, at a large clearing ahead, bear right and keep along the edge to cross a new track to a path on the right of a pond. Cross a stile and continue forward with a hedge on the right to a sandy track which leads out to a road. Turn left for about 200 yards and take the second track on the right by the sign 'Barnsthorns'. Bear right over a stile at the bend by a public footpath notice and bear left immediately. Cross the footbridge into a field. Continue round the edge of the field with lots of bramble bushes on the right. At the entrance to the next field, continue on a path across the corner of the field. Cross another small field and at an entrance turn right on to an enclosed path. Keep on this path, with fine views to the left, and eventually cross a track leading to a large modern house on the right. Continue on this enclosed path to the end of a field. Bear left when a footpath comes in on the right. Take the signposted footpath on the left, ignoring two smaller ones, into the rhododendron and pine woods called the Blue Ride.

Follow this path through the woods for some distance to eventually come out at the bottom of a slope with a field ahead. Turn left at a footpath sign. This path leads out to a road known as The Drift. Turn left and follow the road past The Drift golf course and clubhouse out to Forest Road. Turn right over the railway bridge and then sharp left down Forest Lane, with bungalows on the right. Bear left at a small grassy island in the

35

road. Just before Effingham Common turn right at a public footpath sign through the trees. Follow this path for about a quarter of a mile to a public bridleway sign. Turn sharp left on a short path out to the open common, ignoring a small path on the right. At the common go ahead over a crossing track in an easterly direction towards a line of trees with a short post marked yellow. At the post turn left with trees on the right and at line of trees ahead go through a gap to emerge near the cricket ground. Keep the cricket pitch on the right and come out on a stony lane. Turn left down to the road and turn right for a short distance to turn left down Lower Farm Road, or go diagonally right across the common.

For the shorter walk (4 miles)

From the stile go towards two trees standing alone in the centre of the field. At the trees turn left towards a stile in the hedge. Cross over the stile and turn right down the path. After a National Trust sign, take the first turning on the left through some woods. Cross over a stream and go over the stile into a field. Keep straight ahead on a path between hedge and field and cross under the railway line by the stiles. Continue forward to the end of the next field with a wood ahead, cross a stile and go along the small path with the fine garden of Norwood Farm on the left. This red brick house is thought to have been built six hundred years ago by a Bishop of Winchester as the residence of a bailiff. Cross another stile out on to a small lane, turn left, passing the tithe barn of 103 feet (31 m), and follow the lane to a small common just before the road. Turn left along the edge of the common to join the longer walk at Lower Farm Road.

The two walks continue together as follows. Go down this attractive residential road and at the end climb over the iron ladder into a large field with horses and some large lakes to the far right. Turn left towards the wire fence and at the fence turn right, keeping the fence on the left. Go through a gate at a wire fence, go over a stile and wooden planks and keep to the left edge of the field in the same direction. At the end of the field climb over the large concrete stile and turn immediately left to make for a small path between the railway line and the farm. This enclosed path leads out to a small road. Turn left and cross the railway bridge and follow the road to a large hotel on the corner. Turn right past the hotel and at a sharp bend in the road to the right take the grassy path leading across the common straight ahead. This area is enclosed for cattle grazing. Exit by the gate and take the path to a crossing path. For the car park turn left over a planked bridge and keep to right forks. For the station turn right and cross the footbridge into the station yard.

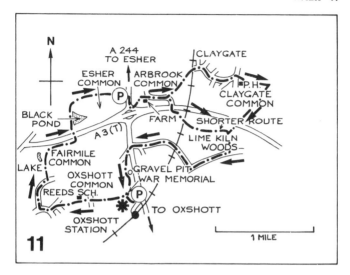

11. Oxshott, Fairmile Common and Claygate

Distance: 6 or 7 miles.
Grid reference: 142611.
Ordnance Survey maps: 1:50,000 sheet 187; 1:25,000 sheet TQ06/16.

This walk crosses some very beautiful commons in the Esher and Claygate area and passes close to two lakes. Some of the paths in the woods will be muddy after rain but the walk is suitable for all seasons and is especially lovely in frosty weather.

Trains: Oxshott station. Walk up towards the Esher-Leatherhead road from the station to the car park on the left-hand side at the top.
Bus: The Mole Valley Leatherhead to Esher bus stops just outside the road leading to Oxshott station. The walk starts from the car park just inside the common.
Car park: The car park is on the right of the Esher-Oxshott-Leatherhead road, coming from Esher, just before the sign to Oxshott station and the railway bridge.
Refreshments: The Winning Horse inn at Claygate is passed on

the longer walk.

The walk starts from the car park on Oxshott Common, which is to the right of the road leading to Oxshott station. From the rear of the car park go forward to cross a bridleway and up a marked path to the War Memorial. Continue along the escarpment, which is provided with seats to admire the fine views across to Fetcham. Descend the steps at the end of the escarpment and turn right at the crossing track. Continue forward across another track until some houses are reached. Go straight ahead through some concrete posts and iron bars to a passage between the houses to the left of another passage, crossing the road after a few yards to a passage opposite. This leads past Reeds School on the left with its fine buildings and playing fields. When the path ends at the corner of a road, continue ahead past a thatched house on the left. Turn right at the end of the road and after about 50 yards turn right down Sandy Lane. At the end of the houses on the right there is a footpath which closely follows the road. At a bend in the road to the right cross the road to a small car park at Fairmile Common.

Take the first path on the right through some posts and at a fork keep to the right. On reaching a crossing track at the corner of a fence, turn right along it. After about 150 yards cross a small stream in a rhododendron dell and climb the slope the other side. Cross over a path and continue along the top of a slope. Descend the slope at the end to reach a beautiful lake in the hollow. Turn right along the bridleway with the motorway on the left, soon on a banked path. At a clear path turn left down the bank and follow the path through the trees to cross the bypass by the footbridge. Turn left and take the first turning on the right through a wooden barrier. After a short while you pass the very lovely Black Pond with its improvised swimming pool, which is no longer in use as the lake is dangerous. Go through some wooden bars and on reaching a crossing path turn right and follow the clear track through the trees. Go under some wooden posts and bear right. At a wide junction of paths, take the second path on the left by a green concrete post. Cross two wide horse rides and at a wooden barrier near the bypass turn half-left. After passing a track coming in on the left, continue forward another 20 yards to bear right at a fork downhill. At a field boundary turn left and take a path on the right still going downhill. Continue towards a car park on the right by Copsem Lane.

Make your way through the car park and cross Copsem Lane to turn right to the roundabout. Turn left down a signed footpath and straight over a crossing track. Go over a little bridge and continue down the path out on to a small road at a corner by a seat. Continue forward past Arbrook Farm and some cottages on the right until reaching a junction of paths. This is where the walks divide.

For the shorter walk (6 miles)

At the junction of paths take the first turning on the right down a sandy track between fields. Go under the bypass by means of the tunnel and keep to the track for about half a mile to reach a T junction. Turn right down to Fairoak Lane. Turn right and after about half a mile turn right down Stokesheath Road. You now rejoin the longer walk at paragraph A.

For the longer walk (7 miles)

At the junction of paths keep on forward through wooden posts. At a fork keep right by fields, soon emerging on a lovely path between fields with open views across to Claygate. This path eventually crosses the railway by a bridge on the outskirts of Claygate. Continue up the small road and turn right along Beaconsfield Road. At the end turn left up to the main road. The Winning Horse is on the right here. Cross the road to go down the small cul-de-sac by the footpath sign and out past the barrier on to Claygate Common. Turn right immediately at a fork and continue in a forward direction to reach a green open space. Cross this to the far left-hand side to a path by some houses. Turn right on a bridlepath, with fields of horses on the left. Continue forward when the common ends at a road. At the end of the road turn left down a footpath to cross the bypass and on for half a mile to Fairoak Lane. Turn right for half a mile to Stokesheath Road on the right. The two walks now continue together.

(A) Turn right down Stokesheath Road and continue along this undulating road with its beautiful houses and lovely views to the right across to Claygate. When the road finally reaches Warren Lane, turn left for about 100 yards to Sandy Lane on the right with a white coal post on the corner of the road. (The coal post, or iron man, with its City of London arms, is a boundary post or coal tax post whose origins go back to Restoration times. In 1667 tolls had to be paid on coal brought into the city and in 1851 the posts were set up at points 20 miles from the GPO but later they were moved and the tolls were abolished in 1889.) Take the path at the corner of the common leading diagonally away between the two roads. When this path reaches the large sand pit, cross the pit and take the path opposite on the left, past a small pond. Continue forward until a bridleway is reached. Turn left along the bridleway which leads round near the road and past the back of the car park.

12. Mickleham, Leatherhead and Fetcham Downs

Distance: 8½ or 5 miles.
Grid reference: 171538.
Ordnance Survey maps: 1:50,000 sheet 187; 1:25,000 sheet TQ15.

This is a lovely walk over Mickleham Downs and the longer walk covers a good stretch of the Roman Stane Street. Both walks finish by crossing Fetcham Downs and Norbury Park, with fine views across the Mole valley. It is suitable for any time of the year.

Trains: Leatherhead station. This adds about another 1½ miles to either walk. From the station go down the approach road and cross the road to a footpath opposite by the Randalls Road sign. Cross a small park with the railway line on the right and, after crossing a road, continue parallel to the railway for about a quarter of a mile. At the main road by the roundabout, go past Bishop and Son down to the Leisure Centre. Bear left between the tennis courts and the football ground and continue through the recreation ground to the river Mole. Turn right and walk along the towpath out through a barrier on to a tarmac drive. Turn right to join the other walk at (*).
Buses: The Green Line bus 714 stops on the A24 just before the turning off to Mickleham.
Car park: The car park is on the left of the A24 (Leatherhead-Dorking road) coming from Leatherhead, about a mile from the roundabout. At a bus stop and telephone kiosk near the sign pointing up the hill to the King William IV public house turn left into Byttom Hill and immediately right to park along the road. There is another car park on the A24 at Leatherhead (see map).
Refreshments: At the King William IV public house (at opening times) and in Leatherhead.

Return to Byttom Hill and turn right up the small rough road. Take the footpath up beside the King William IV pub and when this path emerges on to a crossing track by a broken wall, the walks divide. The shorter walk follows very pleasant roads with beautiful houses and the longer walk goes along Stane Street.
For the shorter walk (5 miles)
Turn left by the broken wall to an iron gate and continue across the junction and on to a fork, where you bear left. Continue on through a white gate and take the next turning on the right up the hill. Turn right up Crabtree Drive by an inset postbox in the wall and eventually emerge on the A24. Cross the road slightly left to a path opposite with posts and follow the attractive lane for

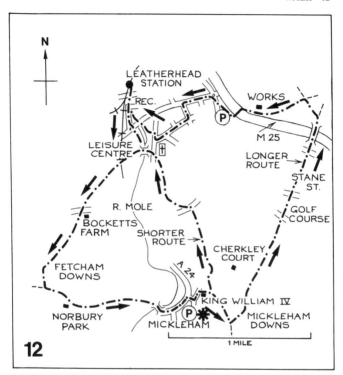

about half a mile. Cross the main road and turn right for a short distance. Turn left down Thorncroft Drive and over the river Mole. (For the station turn right down the towpath and retrace your steps to the station.) Continue the walk at the paragraph headed 'Both walks continue here'.

For the longer walk (8½ miles)

Cross the track to the small path opposite and climb this sloping path through the trees, now badly damaged by the hurricane, to the top. Continue in the same direction on a small path, over a minor crossing path leading to a stile on the left, and 50 yards on, turn left on to a wide stony track for some way to a T junction. Turn left on wide track with wire fences on both sides and keep along Stane Street, which was originally built by the Romans and ran from London to Chichester. Continue on this ancient track, ignoring side turnings, for about two miles, crossing first the main road with Tyrell's Wood golf course on the right and then over two further roads and the M25 by a footbridge. Still continue along Stane Street until reaching a staggered cross track by fields, then turn left. Ignore a small path on the left and at a wide junction of tracks turn left down a magnificent beech avenue, one section of which was ruined by the hurricane, for about half a mile. After passing the extensive Esso complex on the right, turn left and then right on to a path running through a copse. After briefly joining the road at a corner, turn down Green Lane and after a while turn left over the M25 by a walkway and follow the path round to what is left of the original beech avenue. The AA Patrol Service Centre and car park are here.

On reaching the main road, turn right to the roundabout. Cross by the roundabout to take the road leading down towards Leatherhead town centre. (For the station go on down Epsom Road and at the junction cross to the pedestrianised centre of Leatherhead, past the bandstand, and continue in same direction down to cross the river Mole to the roundabout. Turn right back to the station.) To continue the walk, take the second turning on the left, Fortyfoot Road, and then turn right down Poplar Road. This eventually leads past Leatherhead church on the left, with its five-hundred-year-old church tower, out to the main road. Turn left and after a few hundred yards cross the road to Thorncroft Drive on the right. Cross the river Mole.

Both walks continue here

(*)Continue past a mansion and the Leatherhead Leisure Centre. Go over a railway bridge and follow the unmade-up track across a field, through a gate and up the side of another field. Turn left down the other side of the field between hedges and finally out at the bypass. Cross the road to the drive opposite leading to Bocketts Farm, and take the second turning on the right as the drive swings left down to the farm. This path skirts a field and after about half a mile bears round past a barn out to a junction of tracks. Take the small centre track going uphill between bushes with a fine beech tree on the right. At the next crossing track, at a barrier, turn left and cross the main track at the bottom of the slope and continue forward uphill past centuries-old beeches and yews, sadly depleted by the hurricane of 1987. Look out for large London snails, which are the descendants of those brought over by the Romans.

Continue in a forward direction, ignoring all paths to left and right, eventually coming out on to a stony track. Bear left and, on reaching woodcutters' sheds on the right, fork left. At a small lane continue forward on the metalled drive, soon passing Norbury Park House on the right. This house dates from the eighteenth century and is famous for its 'painted room' with walls and ceiling painted with landscapes which blend with the views from the windows. The house now belongs to Surrey County Council.

When the fencing by the side of the track bends to the right, turn right down a small path, crossing a metalled track and continuing on, coming out on to a steep grassy slope covered with violets and cowslips in spring and with fine views across to Mickleham Downs, with Leatherhead to the far left and Box Hill to the right. The Mole at Mickleham in dry summer is sometimes an empty river bed, although a mile away at Burford Bridge it is flowing. The reason is that the waters disappear into the chalk and flow along in subterranean clefts, appearing normally again at Leatherhead.

At the bottom of the slope, keep right of the drive on a pathlet in the grass verge which continues down between posts, and where the track bends left for Mickleham Priory continue straight ahead on the path with a fence on the left and the river Mole on the right, to the bridge and the main road.

Turn left and walk along the A24 and then cross the road to a bus stop and Byttoms Hill turning.

13. Box Hill, Mickleham Downs and White Hill

Distance: 7½ or 5½ miles.
Grid reference: 181513.
Ordnance Survey maps: 1:50,000 sheet 187; 1:25,000 sheet TQ15.

This is a beautiful walk from Box Hill to Juniper Top and the longer walk goes on to Mickleham Downs and the stretch of grassland known as White Hill. This is a hilly walk with at least four ascents (and descents) on the complete walk, two of them being particularly steep. The chalky slopes can be rather slippery after rain but this is a walk for any season although the flaming colours of the foliage on the downs in autumn are particularly striking.

Trains: West Humble and Box Hill BR station. From the station go down the approach road to the A24. Cross by the subway and turn left to the Burford Bridge Hotel. Climb the steep side of Box Hill and at the top turn right on to a chalky track keeping the escarpment on the right. After passing Labelliere's tomb, turn left away from the edge at a fork, and go through some posts to the Fort tea rooms and car park opposite.

Bus: Green line bus 714 stops on the A24, either at Burford Bridge hotel (see directions for trains) or near the King William IV pub (go up the small road by the side of the bus stop and ignore a right fork almost immediately — start the walk from A).

Car park: National Trust car park opposite the Fort tea rooms on the top of Box Hill.

Refreshments: At the King William IV public house (at opening times) and on the top of Box Hill when the Fort tea rooms are open (on the longer walk).

From the National Trust car park opposite the Fort tea rooms cross the green to another car park by the side of the road. Keeping the road on the right, follow a faint track in the woods and cross a tarmac drive leading to a house. Continue forward to reach a T junction with a fence ahead to a caravan park. Turn left, and at the corner of the fence turn right by the National Trust sign and follow the path past two side paths marked by NT posts to reach eventually a stile by a stone memorial seat. Cross the open downland called Juniper Top with fine views across to Mickleham Downs and beyond, and go downhill to enter a wooded area at Juniper Bottom and emerge at a small road by a cottage.

Cross the road and climb the very steep slope opposite. Bear to the right on the main path in an uphill direction until you reach a well placed seat with fine views across the valley to Ranmore church.

For the shorter walk (5½ miles)

Take the lower path to the right of the seat and, after descending a slope with a field ahead, bear round to the left and out to a car park.

For the longer walk (7½ miles)

Continue past the seat in the same direction. At a black iron corner post turn left and after about 40 yards fork left by another iron post and keep on the main path, which drops down to a wide track (Stane Street). Cross to the 'squeeze' in the wire fence ahead and follow the path downhill. Cross the stile at the end of the path and continue along a gravelled drive to take the second gate on the right through the churchyard by the beautiful Mickleham church. Keep on forward on a path between a fence and a hedge, crossing a track to a path opposite. Turn right at a garden just before the main road ahead and continue forward to come out to a road where you turn right up to the King William

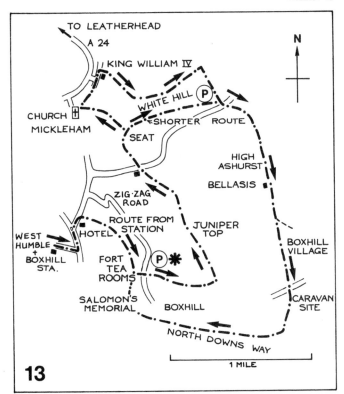

13

IV pub.

(**A**) Take the footpath up the side of the pub, crossing a track to a small path opposite. This path wends its way up through ancient yews and beeches (now much depleted by the October 1987 hurricane). After some way ignore a path on the right and cross over a track shortly afterwards. At a sloping cross junction cross to the footpath opposite. At the end of the fence on the right, turn right on a wide track which eventually leads round to the left on to White Hill. Turn left along this wide stretch of grassland to the end and go past a National Trust signpost, almost immediately branching off to the right just before a fence for a nature reserve. Keep ahead when the path divides to the right. This beautiful woodland path soon steepens downhill and the last slopes can be slippery after rain. It emerges at a small road by the side of a car park, with a cottage opposite.

45

The two walks continue together

Cross the road to the bridleway by the side of the cottage and continue up this path with fields on either side. At the end of an old flint wall, keep ahead along the metalled road. In winter there are fine views to the left across to Headley Heath. After passing the entrance to Ashurst Youth Camp on the right, there is a horse ride on the left which closely follows the road initially, but when it swings away from the road take a right turning back to the road. Leave the road at a junction of paths, keeping to the track nearest the woods on the right. The track passes some houses and caravans on the outskirts of Box Hill village and finally comes out to a road with the 'Roof of the World' caravan site across the road on the left. Cross the road to the footpath opposite and follow the path past a riding school on the right until it joins the North Downs Way, denoted by the acorn sign.

The disused Brockham Quarries can be seen away to the left. Follow the acorn signs down some staggered steps across the path and then turn sharply to the right up some steps and a steep slope with a hand rail, still following the North Downs Way. On reaching a track at a horseshoe bend, take the right-hand path leading uphill. At a gate turn left down some steps and follow the acorn signs and white marks on the trees, eventually coming out on the fine escarpment of Box Hill. Walk along the open downland, keeping the road on the right, until you reach the pulpit on Box Hill built in memory of Leopold Salomons of Norbury Park, who gave Box Hill to the nation in 1914. The famous view here over the Weald to Chanctonbury Ring and the South Downs is unforgettable. The Fort tea rooms and car park are a little further on.

14. South Holmwood and Anstiebury Farm

Distance: 7 or 5 miles.
Grid reference: 172451.
Ordnance Survey maps: 1:50,000 sheet 187; 1:25,000 sheet TQ14.

A walk over Holmwood Common to Fourwents Pond and then along fields and woodland paths up to Anstiebury Farm on the Redland Heights, where there are splendid views across Surrey. The longer walk continues along the Heights and then down to cross the main road to Holmwood Common, whilst the shorter walk returns to the car park via South Holmwood.

Trains: From Holmwood station turn left and take the first

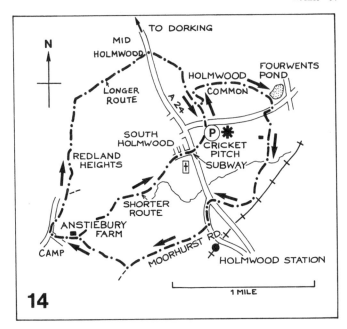

14

1 MILE

turning on the left, Moorhurst Lane, to join the walk at (*).
Buses: Buses from Dorking stop near the war memorial in South
Holmwood on the A24. Turn up Mill Road to join the walk at the
car park.
Car park: On the A24, Dorking to Horsham road, take the
turning, Mill Road, on the left from Dorking in South Holmwood
village and park in one of the small car parks on either side of the
road, about 100 yards from the main road.
Refreshments: Public houses on the A24.

From either car park go 30 yards further on down the road to
take the path on the left by a public footpath sign. After about a
quarter of a mile, when the hedge and drive of a house appear
ahead, turn left on to a smaller path over a plank bridge.
Continue on the main rising path to a crossing track and turn
right to take a small path to the left of the house ahead. After
passing a dried-up pond carry on forward a short distance up to a
T junction. Turn right along a grassy track, cross a horseride and
immediately turn right down a wide grassy track parallel to the

horse ride. Follow this wide track over a planked stream to pass through two horse barriers. After the second, turn right downhill to follow telegraph wires. Cross over a planked stream and continue over a crossing track. In 20 yards turn left on a path, soon with a small stream on the right. In 150 yards turn right and cross the stream. Continue forward about 15 yards to a fork. Take the right-hand path slightly uphill to a small crossing track. Turn left by a holly bush towards the attractive Fourwents Pond, with plenty of seats for picnickers. Look out for Muscovy and other ducks and geese. At the pond turn right through the car park to Mill Road.

Turn right along Mill Road for a short distance and then turn left down a drive marked with a public bridleway sign. At the end of the houses climb over a stile to continue on the concrete path between fields. After crossing a brick bridge over a stream carry on up the slope of the field on a small indistinct grassy path. At the top of the slope bear half-right to a small gate in the line of trees about 75 yards from the railway line. (There may be electric fences dividing the fields but the farmer has provided stiles.) Go through the gate and at the crossing track turn right. Ignore a left fork and at some cottages bordering a small green, join a made-up lane to the main road ahead.

Cross the dual carriageway to a small road slightly to the left, signposted Beare Green. After a short way turn right down Moorhurst Lane to Moorhurst Manor.

(*)After about half a mile, just after a drive down to a house on the left, keep forward on the rising track past a 'no through road' sign. After another half a mile, when the path becomes tree-lined, turn right over a barrier with a PF sign.

Climb up the side of the field, keeping the hedge on the right, and go through a gap in the top right-hand corner. Follow the path half left across the middle of the field to a stile by the edge of a wood. Continue along the path through the beechwood (devastated by the 1987 hurricane) with a wire fence on the right. Where the track bears left carry on ahead up to another stile. Cross the field diagonally right to a stile situated to the right of some farm buildings on the skyline. This is Anstiebury Farm and the walks diverge here.

For the shorter walk (5 miles)

Turn right along the rough farm track with its superb views and by the entrance to a house called Taresmocks cross a stile ahead by the side of a wall. Continue down this path, which eventually comes out on to a small road. Turn left along it to the main road, ignoring a road to the left and passing the church away on the right. Cross under the main road by means of the subway, climb the steps past the war memorial and continue round the cricket pitch to the car park.

For the longer walk (7 miles)

Turn left through the farm and at the minor road turn right. (The site of Anstiebury Camp — an Iron Age hill fortress — is on the left.) At the T junction turn right and after 100 yards turn right on to a rising path. Continue on this path ignoring side turnings. Continue forward when gravel track joins from the left and at a fork bear right on the gravel track to reach a large water tank at a meeting of paths. Take the second path on the left going forward. This path soon bends to the right and continues downhill. Ignore a left turn going steeply downhill. Our path soon steepens and descends. Go over crossing tracks and under telegraph poles, and then take a left fork. Cross a wooden barrier and bend left to some cottages. Go round the hedge of a cottage on to a track which leads down to the main road.

Cross the main road with great care to the bridleway opposite on Holmwood Common. After crossing a planked stream bear right at a T junction. Ignore tracks coming in from the left and at a clearing with a bench by an oak, bend sharply right and go over crossing tracks. After passing a defunct football pitch on the right, ignore a path bending to the right round the top of the pitch and go ahead on a path which curves round to a metal barrier. Go under the barrier and turn right after about 200 yards at the first crossing track, leading downhill into a gully. Cross the stream and climb up the other side. At the top of the rise bear right. This track soon joins the outward path to return to the car park. For the station, turn left on joining the path and continue from the first paragraph of the walk 'when the hedge and drive of a house appear ahead.'

15. Highridge Wood, Brockham and Betchworth

Distance: 7½ miles.
Grid reference: 198470.
Ordnance Survey maps: 1:50,000 sheet 187; 1:25,000 sheets TQ14, TQ24.

A delightful walk through woodland and fields to Brockham, then on to the outskirts of Betchworth, returning via Gadbrook. There are no hills to climb and for the most part it is easy walking country except for some rather dilapidated stiles, but some mud will be encountered in the winter months. Many of the footpaths are across farm land and care should be taken not to damage any of the crops and to keep dogs under control.

Bus: 439 (Newdigate-Redhill) and 449. No services on Sunday. The nearest bus stop is at the crossroads about 1½ miles south of Brockham. Turn right at the crossroads and after a few hundred yards turn right to the Forestry Commission car park in Highridge Wood.

Car park: In Highridge Wood. Take the road to Brockham from the A25 and at a crossroads 1½ miles south of Brockham turn right. The car park is a few hundred yards down the road on the right.

Refreshments: Inns and shops at Brockham and an inn at Betchworth.

In the Forestry Commission car park in Highridge Wood, take the main track opposite the car park entrance through the dark pinewood. At the end of the wood by some wooden posts cross the clearing to a wide track opposite. Continue ahead on this track and eventually go down a gentle slope to the remains of a stile on to a smaller grassy path. A few yards on, at a little grassy triangle on the right, take the path into trees on the right, later by a ditch on the left. Shortly, at a T junction, turn left and go for about 20 yards to a field ahead passing through horizontal poles. Keep forward along the right-hand edge of the field by the hedge and go through a gate on to a rough track leading past a house by a lane. Turn right, and then left down a small road past a farm. At a corner of the lane, shortly before a cottage on the right, turn right through a gate on a rough track across a field. Cross Tanners Brook and immediately bear off diagonally right to a gate and stile in the corner of the field. Now keep ahead along the edge of various fields, crossing over some stiles and other barriers, until you come to a farm track by a farm. Turn right towards Brockham and at the road turn left, shortly crossing a bridge, into Brockham village, with its beautiful green and picturesque cottages and inns. This is one of the most photographed village cricket greens in England and W. G. Grace is said to have played there. On Guy Fawkes night a huge bonfire and fireworks display are held on the green.

Cross the road to a small road opposite, past the Royal Oak and Duke's Head public houses, and shortly take the public bridleway ahead to the left of a drive to a house. Cross the river Mole and keep to the right along the lane. At a fork by a hedge, keep right past some back gardens at first, with the river below on the right. At the end of a field cross to a footpath ahead and at some farm buildings keep ahead past a notice saying 'Beware of the bull'. This path leads past Betchworth church and through an arch to a lane.

Cross to the road opposite with the Dolphin inn on the corner. Follow this road for about a mile, passing More Place, a restored

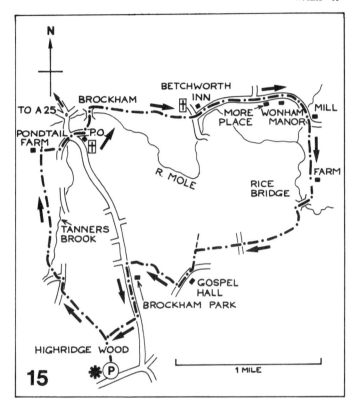

fifteenth-century house with a stone chimneystack at the north end, and soon glimpsing Wonham Manor with its battlements. At Wonham Mill on the left, turn right over a very narrow foot-bridge over the Mole. Follow the path through the woods, cross a stile and keep along a wire fence bordering the river. Here the first of at least four pillboxes can be seen on the left. Turn left along the riverside and follow the path up between telegraph posts. Cross a stile and continue along the path on the left-hand side of the field, past a further pillbox, and skirt a garden. Go ahead to a metal gate with wooden bars on both sides. Turn right along the sunken path, which leads to the river once more by the fourth pillbox.

Cross the river by the concrete bridge and take the footpath slightly uphill ahead. Go through posts into a large field and keep to the right-hand edge of the field. At the top of the field turn left and continue along with a wood on the right to an iron gate and track into a wood. At the far end of the wood keep along the right-hand side of a field to a stile in the corner out on to a small road. Cross slightly left to a footpath sign opposite and continue across the middle of this large field. At a cart track halfway across the field, continue in the same direction to a track. Turn left up towards a house on the far edge of the field. At the house continue on a track leading to a road with a chapel opposite. Turn right and in a short distance turn right again opposite Hall Farm at a public footpath sign. At a cottage ahead take a small footpath on the left past a garage, cross a stile and keep along the right-hand hedgerow to cross a bridge and stile. Turn left and follow the edge of the field to a further stile. Continue ahead along the left-hand edge of a field to a stile out on to a road. Buses stop on this road. Turn left up the road past the entrance to Brockham Park and up the hill. Go past cottages on the right and take a path over a stile on the right at footpath sign. Go ahead along right-hand edge of field to corner, cross wooden posts and go straight ahead through a copse, emerging at bridleway past and wide crossing track. Cross this to the small track opposite. Ignore the first turning on the left and at the next junction, at a fork, branch left on a wide grassy ride, passing bridleway signs, and in a small clearing take the narrow path slightly right ahead, through the posts to re-enter the pinewoods and so retrace one's steps to the car park.

16. Chessington and Epsom Common

Distance: 5½ miles.
Grid reference: 179634.
Ordnance Survey maps: 1:50,000 sheet 187; 1:25,000 sheets TQ06/16, TQ15.

This walk takes you across farm land and the Horton Country Park to the large stew ponds on Epsom Common and returns via the outskirts of Chessington World of Adventures and Winey Hill.

Trains: Chessington South station.
Bus: Number 71 (Richmond, Kingston, Chessington) stops outside the station.

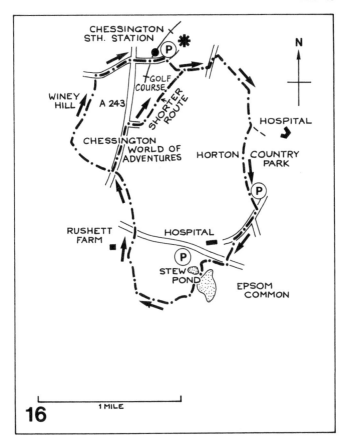

16 1 MILE

Car park: There is a car park at Chessington South station and also at Horton Country Park and by the stew ponds on Epsom Common. See map for locations.

From the station turn left and after about 50 yards turn right up a footpath between some houses. Continue on this path until you reach open land with fine views across to Epsom and Ashtead Commons. Turn left on a path with the golf course down on the right and, keeping houses on the left, continue forward to a small road. Turn left for 100 yards to a footpath on the right opposite a four-storey block of flats. This path leads

53

down past a noisy dogs' boarding kennels, over a barred fence and across a bridge. Continue forward along the edge of a field, cross a stile and ahead to the top of the next field. Go round the field to the right, ignore the first gap and, after a short distance, there is a stile in the trees on the left. Cross this to follow a small path and continue forward when this soon meets a wide track. This is the Horton Country Park.

After about a quarter of a mile bear slightly right by a white house and continue on for another half a mile or so on a wide track, through a six-barred gate and out to a wide crossing track. Go through a narrow gap in the wooden fencing opposite and continue ahead, soon by a fence, and turn left past the car park out to a road.

Turn right up the road, bear right at a fork and when the road bends right into a hospital, continue forward along a bridle track. At the end of the track cross the road to a path leading into Epsom Common. After about 50 yards, at a T junction, turn right on a cinder track which leads through woods to a meadow with the stew pond on the left. The car park off the B280 is on the right.

At the meadow turn left and skirt the pond on the right. At the head of the pond bear left to a flight of steps leading to the upper stew pond which is a wildlife reserve. Turn right and continue forward. At a crossing track turn right and after 20 yards turn left and keep on the main path in a generally westerly direction to meet a cinder track. Turn right and in 50 yards turn left on a small path. Go over a crossing track and turn right at a T junction towards fields. At footpath signs turn left to another set of footpath signs by a coal post. These were boundary posts erected in 1851 to mark the edge of the Metropolitan Police District, where tolls on coal and wine brought into London were levied.

Turn right and cross the field slightly right on the track and continue on to Rushett Lane. Cross to a signed path opposite and follow this path to the main road by Chessington World of Adventures. (On reaching the road by the World of Adventures a short cut back to the station and bus can be taken by turning right past World of Adventures to Chalky Lane on the right. After passing the football club ground turn left through metal posts at a bend in the lane. After about half a mile the path joins a track which soon becomes a metalled road. At the end of the golf course turn left by a footpath sign and cross the end of the course to reach the outward path between the houses. Turn left at the road for the station, bus and car park.)

For the return past Chessington World of Adventures, cross the main road to a footpath signposted to Claygate. Follow the perimeter of the World of Adventures up the hill to the next footpath sign, where you turn right by the circus. There are fine views here across to Claygate and the new lake by the side of the Esher bypass. The World of Adventures (formerly Chessington Zoo) occupies the site of Burnt Stub, a fourteenth-century house burned down to a 'stub' by Parliamentarians during the Civil War. Continue on through a wooden enclosure on to Winey Hill. With the fence on the right, cross the hill to a little lane by Barwell Court. Turn right and continue on to the main road. Cross to Garrison Lane opposite and on to Chessington South station.

17. Reigate Hill, Gatton Park and Merstham

Distance: 6 or 7 miles.
Grid reference: 263523.
Ordnance Survey maps: 1:50,000 sheet 187; 1:25,000 sheet TQ25.

This walk follows the North Downs Way to the east from Reigate Hill, through Gatton Park, to Merstham and returns on the other side of the motorway through fields and lanes.

Trains: From the station at Merstham turn left up Station Road to the main road. Turn right to the corner by the Feathers and take the road ahead marked 'No through road'. Continue the walk at the paragraph marked (*).

Buses: The 405, 414, 440 and 455 buses stop in Merstham. Follow the directions from the Feathers as above. Alternatively, the 406 and 422 buses to Redhill stop after the large roundabout on the A217 just before Reigate Hill. Cross Gatton Bottom Lane to the National Trust and North Downs Way signs on the left of Wray Lane opposite the car park.

Car park: After the large roundabout on the A217 over the M25, fork left then immediately right to the car park in Wray Lane at the top of Reigate Hill.

Refreshments: In the car park on Reigate Hill or in Merstham.

From the car park cross Wray Lane at the entrance of the car park to the North Downs Way signpost and follow the path to the right down the hill. A very pleasant extra mile's walking can be taken at this point through the wood.

For the longer walk

When the path bends to the left continue forward down to a wood. Cross over a track and go on with fence on the left to a gate, and on up the hill. Bear round to the left and then swing right on a wide track down the hill. At the bottom of the hill turn left passing riding buildings on the right. Keep ahead, ignoring the rising path on the left, to an enclosed track with views of Gatton Park Lake and beyond. Go through a gate to the top of the rise to join the North Downs Way by turning right through Gatton Park on a tarmac drive.

The shorter walk continues on the main path to the bottom of the hill and at the cottage at the bottom turn right down a metalled lane passing the Royal Alexandra and Albert School and Hospital in Gatton Park. (Gatton Hall was once owned by the Colman family of mustard fame.)

Both walks now follow the North Downs Way sign at the chapel by turning left to North Lodge gate. Go forward on the road round the bend to the North Downs Way sign, and turn left down the drive. Go past houses and small nursery on the right. At the end of the nursery by an old gate take the footpath on the left between fences, climb the stile into some fruit fields and continue forward parallel to the M25 and on diagonally downhill across a field to a signposted stile, past Merstham cricket ground into Merstham itself.

(*)Turn left along the aptly named Quality Street, which was once part of the old road to Croydon until the present road was built in 1807. It is said to owe its present name to a reference to Barrie's play of the same name in which Sir Seymour Hicks and his wife, Ellaline Terriss, were acting. They lived in the Old Forge House, which is marked as a building of special interest at the end of the street on the right. Turn down the passage beside it, crossing the motorway by the footbridge to the lane ahead.

We now leave the North Downs Way by crossing this lane to some stone steps opposite. Go through the wooden gate and turn sharp left up some steps, skirting the church on the right. Follow the path to some steps up on to a lane. Turn left and just before a white house on the left, about 150 yards, turn left on to a footpath. In November hundreds of pheasants could be seen in the fields and woods here. After a while cross two stiles close together and then go diagonally left across a field to a farm and barn in the hollow. Cross a stile at the left end of the hedge and turn right along the edge of the field to a stile leading out to a minor road. Turn left along the road for nearly three-quarters of a mile, passing a fine house on the right. At a T junction turn left for about 25 yards to a stile in the hedge on the right. Cross the stile and walk up the left-hand side of the field to a stile in the corner. Continue in the same direction with a coppice now on the right to cross a stile at the next corner. On entering a wood keep on in the same direction — bluebells are abundant here — past a pillbox and over another stile. Continue forward with views of Upper Gatton Park on the left, over a further stile and finally out to a lane by a cottage.

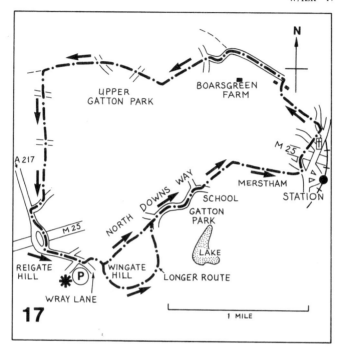

N

UPPER
GATTON PARK

BOARSGREEN
FARM

A 217

M 25

NORTH DOWNS WAY

MERSTHAM

SCHOOL

STATION

GATTON
PARK

LAKE

M 25

REIGATE
HILL

WINGATE
HILL

LONGER ROUTE

WRAY LANE

17

1 MILE

Cross the road to a stile in the hedge and keep on in the same direction, passing a clump of trees on the right. Keep the wire fence on the right and at the end of the field cross the stile to another stile over the road, to the left of a cottage with a very pretty garden. Follow the path over three stiles and at the end of a fence on the right, cut diagonally left across the field to a gate and farm track. Turn left to the farm, go through the gate and turn right up a stony track to a public footpath sign at the top. Turn left over a stile, continue over further stiles past some fine houses out on to a road. Cross this to a kissing gate opposite and cross the field with the hedge on the left. Go over a stile and continue in the same direction towards a small but beautifully kept mobile homes park. Cross the stile to take the path running alongside the caravans out to a road. Cross Blackhorse Lane and walk along the main A217 road towards the roundabout. Cross the M25 slip road and walk across the bridge over the M25. Turn left up the main Reigate road past the bus stop and cross Gatton Bottom Lane to Wray Lane with the car park on the right.

18. Caterham, Arthur's Seat and Paddock Barn

Distance: 7 miles.
Grid reference: 337554.
Ordnance Survey maps: 1:50,000 sheet 187; 1:25,000 sheet TQ35.

A lovely walk from Caterham following the North Downs Way over White Hill and Gravelly Hill with superb views to the south on a clear day, returning to Caterham via field paths.

Trains: Caterham station. From the station entrance turn right up Church Hill to St Mary's church on the right at the top. The footpath entrance is by a bus stop on the left just past the church.
Buses: 409 and 411 buses stop just past St Mary's church, or 197 in Caterham. Follow the directions from the station.
Car park: There is parking in side roads near St Mary's church on the B2030, Caterham, or free parking at Caterham station at weekends or in a car park just off the roundabout in Caterham. There is also parking for a few cars at Gravelly Hill (see map.)
Refreshments: In Caterham or at the inn near Arthur's Seat.

The walk starts by turning left down the footpath by the bus stop which is just past St Mary's church on the top of Church Hill, Caterham. Opposite St Mary's church is the ancient downland church of St Lawrence, which is still used for some services. The path is enclosed by laurel hedges and railings at first but soon emerges at a large recreation park (toilets here on the right by the tennis courts). Keep on the path ahead, which runs alongside the back gardens of some houses, and at the end of the park continue through a wooden barrier in the same direction past a small cul-de-sac and on another enclosed path with a fine open space on the left. Go down through another barrier and cross the road to a pleasant residential avenue opposite going gently uphill. At the end of this avenue turn left and then right down Birchwood Lane. This lane soon leaves houses behind to continue with fields on either side. When it peters out turn left at a signpost and keep on this path with a fence on the left to go through barriers into a field. Cross the field on the enclosed path and out to a track.

Turn left along the North Downs Way and at a farm turn right on a footpath leading past the farm and an old barn on to a metalled track between fields. Go through a gate to continue on a cart track. Where the path goes steeply downhill at the corner of the field, keep left between a field and a hedge, then bear right through brick gateposts out on to a road. There is a pub up the road to the left.

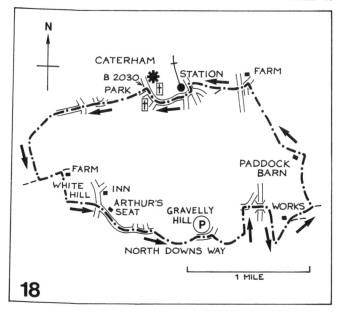

Cross to the road opposite, soon passing a folly tower on the left called Arthur's Seat. Continue along the North Downs Way, which follows this road for about three quarters of a mile to some crossroads, and take the North Downs Way footpath, which is half-right and starts behind the Hextalls Lane sign. Keep on this path for some way, eventually passing through some green posts, and follow the acorn signs out on to a road past the viewpoint at Gravelly Hill, where there is some parking. Turn right by the North Downs Way sign into woods and continue to follow the acorns and blue signs for about half a mile, ignoring side turnings into the valley, until the path comes out on to a small road.

Turn right down the road and when it bends to the left to join the dual carriageway in the valley, turn right by a post to cross the road by the footbridge. Cross the stile ahead to a further stile and turn right, still on the North Downs Way. After about 100 yards bear left by a stile and follow the path out to a road. Cross this to a path opposite and when this path emerges at a track with a house on the right leave the North Downs Way to take the path ahead steeply uphill through the woods with a large works on the left. Continue uphill for some way to cross a wire fence with wooden slats and bear left following a small path to a huge fallen beech tree. Go over a stile on the left into a field and keep forward uphill with a wire fence on the left. At the corner of the field cross over railings and keep a fence to a field on the right to pass some farm buildings. Turn left at the end of the farm and follow the track past a corrugated iron fence on the left. At the end of the fence turn right and continue on this cart track for about a mile on a wide ridge with good views to left and right. On reaching some buildings, turn left and left again down a drive.

When the drive nears the dual carriageway, branch off to the right on a short track and down stone steps to cross through the barrier of the busy main road to a stone footpath sign opposite. Follow the path down towards Caterham and, where it forks, keep right alongside a wire fence. Eventually the path bends round to the left down to Commonwealth Road. Keep forward into Caterham. Turn left to the roundabout and then right past the station. Church Hill is on the right.

Index